ISLAND OF
COZUMEL

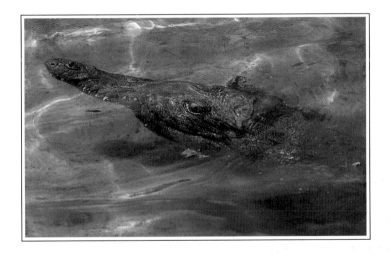

185 full color photographs

Photography by Luis Gómez C.

PUBLICADO POR EDITORA FOTOGRAFICA MARINA KUKULCAN, CANCUN, MEXICO

ISLA DE

MAR

ISLA MUJERES

PUNTA SUR

PLAYA NORTE

PARQUE MARINO NACIONAL ARRECIFES DE CANCUN

PUNTA SAM

PUERTO JUAREZ

EL MECO

ZONA HOTELERA

ZONA HOTELERA

CANCUN

LAGUNA NICHUPTE

PUNTA NIZUC

CIUDAD CANCUN

B A R R I E R   R E E F

AEROPUERTO INTERNACIONAL DE CANCUN

PUERTO MORELOS

RODMAN (Astillero)

ADUANA

CENTRAL VALLARTA

PUNTA MAROMA

Map of Cozumel and the coast of Quintana Roo taken from a satellite photograph.

CARRETERA LIBRE

SUPERCARRETERA DE CUOTA

a MERIDA

GOLFO DE MEXICO

FLORIDA

BAHAMAS

CUBA

PENINSULA DE YUCATAN

COZUMEL

MAR CARIBE

JAMAICA

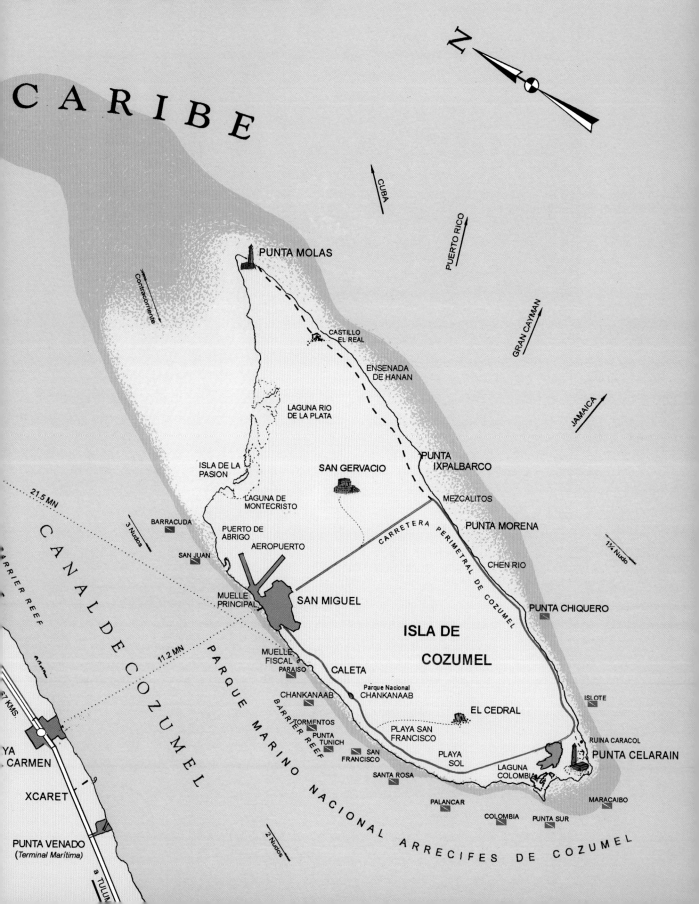

COZUMEL

CARIBE

N

CUBA

PUERTO RICO

GRAN CAYMAN

JAMAICA

Contracorriente

PUNTA MOLAS

CASTILLO
EL REAL

ENSENADA
DE HANAN

LAGUNA RIO
DE LA PLATA

21.5 MN

ISLA DE LA
PASION

SAN GERVACIO

PUNTA
IXPALBARCO

BARRACUDA

3 Nudos

LAGUNA DE
MONTECRISTO

MEZCALITOS

PUNTA MORENA

1¾ Nudo

PUERTO DE
ABRIGO

SAN JUAN

AEROPUERTO

CHEN RIO

CARRETERA PERIMETRAL DE COZUMEL

CANAL DE COZUMEL

BARRIER REEF

MUELLE
PRINCIPAL

SAN MIGUEL

PUNTA CHIQUERO

11.2 MN

PARQUE MARINO NACIONAL ARRECIFES DE COZUMEL

MUELLE
FISCAL

PARAISO

CALETA

ISLA DE

COZUMEL

57 KMS.

BARRIER REEF

CHANKANAAB

Parque Nacional
CHANKANAAB

EL CEDRAL

ISLOTE

YA
CARMEN

TORMENTOS

PUNTA
TUNICH

SAN
FRANCISCO

Playa San
FRANCISCO

PLAYA
SOL

RUINA CARACOL

PUNTA CELARAIN

XCARET

SANTA ROSA

LAGUNA
COLOMBIA

PUNTA VENADO
(Terminal Marítima)

a TULUM

2 Nudos

PALANCAR

COLOMBIA

PUNTA SUR

MARACAIBO

CONTENTS

INTRODUCTION

The purpose of this book as both guide and souvenir, is to help you plan your visits and maximize your memories of all that is Cozumel. The remarkable images of award winning photographer, Luis Gomez stir the imagination and refresh the spirit. The spectacular clarity and color of the waters surrounding the island of Cozumel and the amazing panorama just beneath the surface await your personal experience.

Tourism is nothing new to Cozumel. Over a thousand years ago the Putun Maya did a brisk business in pilgrims. At least once in their life Maya women journeyed to Cozumel's temple of Ixchel, goddess of weaving and childbirth. As the post-classic Maya population is reckoned in the millions, there must have been a constant crossing of canoes to Cozumel from the ancient port of Pole (modern Xcaret). These intrepid Maya traders were the Phoenicians of the New World, and Cozumel was their home port. Whether you come by cruise ship for shopping and relaxation or arrive by air for a dive expedition, don't neglect to see the temples of San Gervasio, or the charming little "Caracol" on Punta Celarain. The remaining landmarks of Maya legacy are not to be missed.

Cozumel is rich in history. The Carib Indians were displaced by what became the paragon of culture in the New World. The only Amerind society to develop writing; Maya astronomy, botanical medicine and mathematics were superior to that of the Europeans. After a peaceful landing, the first mass in Mexico was celebrated on the beach at San Miguel in 1518. Depredation began immediately with Old World diseases halving the original population of 20,000 in 80 years. De facto slavery and piracy did the rest, and by the 17th century the island was abandoned. The only visitors were turtles and the occasional English freebooter seeking a deserted cove to bury his hoard. Re-population began with refugees from the "War of the Castes" in 1840's. Their exports of chicle and coconut products brought contact with the U.S. and Britain via Belize. The 1920's saw regular airline service and the return of travelers like Charles Lindbergh. The island's fame as a premier dive destination began in the 1950's with a visit from Jacques Cousteau to Palancar. His popularization of the reef's spectacular marine life began the touristic boom for the Mexican Caribbean. From the first Cruise ships in the 1960's, 800 luxury liners with 1,000,000 passengers now make the island the 2nd most popular cruise stop in the Caribbean and 5th in the world.

With all its modern conveniences, Cozumel has not lost its small island feel and tranquil charm, still retaining the natural beauty which made it famous. Nearly the entire reef has been made into National Parks in which all marine life is protected. The calendar of fiestas runs all year, each reflecting different aspects of Island culture. The annual Spring migration of marlin and sailfish makes for world class fishing in the waters just offshore. The flat calms of summer expand the range of fantastic diving. One needn't go to great depths or even get wet for the sight of a queen angel fish, giant sponges or graceful sea anemones. There are glass bottom boats, complete diver certification courses and in 20 minutes you can be a nearly expert snorkeler and viewing aquatic marvels 10 yards from the shore!

photo 1. Panorama of the north of Cozumel showing the lighthouse on Punta Molas and the dangerous reefs. In the background, Rio de Plata.

The island of Cozumel derives its name from the Mayan word Cuzamil, land of the swallows. It is the largest island in the Mexican Caribbean and most populated island of Mexico. Located east of the Yucatan Peninsula from which it is separated by a 18 kilometer wide canal, it is Mexico's eastern most territory and is truly a window to the Caribbean.

Its longest point stretches north to south, measuring 52 kilometers and its narrowest point east to west is just 14 kilometers across. The total superficies is just over 500 square kilometers.

Like the majority of the Yucatan Peninsula, Cozumel's geological origin pertains to the Pliocene epoch, being part of the earth forms that emerged from the sea during the final phase of the Tertiary period. Its rocky foundation is made up of marine sediment and its outer superficies often contains noticeable fossil incrustations. Calculations date its age at 16 million years.

photo 2 Possessing great natural beauty and rarely visited by tourists, the northeastern side of the island is a coastal route that includes Mayan worship sites by the sea, ample white sand beaches and rocky inlets. This photo shows the road passing by Punta Ixpalbarco.

photo 3 The reef is home to a variety of schools of fish, like the yellow snapper and grunts that inhabit this site known as Bolones de Chankanaab.

photo 4 Aerial view of the southern part of Cozumel showing the beaches near the lighthouse on Punta Celarain, Colombia Lagoon and in the background Chunchakab Cove and the southern point of the island.

Aerial view of the Hannan reefs on the east coast of Cozumel.

Its astronomical location between 20º and 20º 45' latitude north place it in the heart of the tropical zone producing a sub-humid climate with abundant rains distributed throughout the year. There are no marked dry and wet seasons and in spite of the abundant fluvial activity, the island does not have a large visible water supply. Due to the high permeability of the soil, there are no rivers or permanent superficial water deposits. Instead the island's water supply, like that of the peninsula's is found in networks of subterranean currents and deposits commonly known as cenotes. The beauty of the caverns and tunnels that time has sculpted in these underwater deposits as well as the incredible transparency of the water make them

privileged sites for experienced divers.

Steggerda's classification of the soils of the peninsula, in which he utilized Mayan terms, classifies the island as "Tzekel", calcareous rock covered with a thin layer of soil. The high level of lime in the stone is what creates the excessively permeable nature of the ground facilitating the formation of caverns. It is also the reason for the white sands of the beaches and the extreme clarity and luminosity of the coastal waters. The thin layer of soil creates a jungle vegetation that is classified as semi-deciduous growth.

5

Like all tropical vegetation, Cozumel's is varied and abundant. The maximum height of trees does not surpass 25 meters and is made up predominately of zapote, ramon, ceiba, chit, jabin, caracolillo, guaya and chechen, as well as shrubbery such as icaco, and resinosa. In the swamplands, tasiste, red mangrove, white mangrove and Botoncillo can be found.

Cultivated plants native to the tropics such as pineapple, mamey, citrus, mango, watermelon, banana, etc. produce abundant crops although in recent years the cultivation of these and other traditional crops such as corn, bean, squash, chile, sweet potato, etc. have been somewhat abandoned as farmers seek more profitable activities within the tourism sector. The same can be said for orchards and flower growing, which in spite of their abundant yield, are rarely cultivated at present.

The wildlife, although diminished due to years of hunting (now prohibited), is still notable and an assortment of animals can still be found in the jungle including: hares, badgers, raccoons, armadillos, tepezcuintle, mountain boars and occasionally deer. There are no felines, though snakes do exist, none of a poisonous nature. Alligators also thrive in the swamplands.

photo 1 & 5, In the highest branches of the dry trees the frigate bird takes shelter from the alligators. The Rio de la Plata Lagoon is home to Acutus and Moreleti crocodiles whose diet consists of marine birds, fish, badgers and crabs.

photo 7 Protected from the indiscriminate hunting that almost eliminated them on the island, crocodiles now enjoy a safe refuge in Punta Sur Park where they live and reproduce free from human disturbances.

photo 2 & 4 Covered with mangrove and almost completely destroyed, the ruins of Rio de la Plata Lagoon are a display of Mayan culture from days past.

photo 3 The ancient Mayan route is easy to make out even beneath the waters of the lagoon.

photo 6 The white heron is one of the species that inhabit the lagoons on the eastern side of Cozumel.

7

With respect to avian fauna the jungle is home to parrots, wild doves, pheasants, turtledoves, and of course, the swallows which are the namesake of the island and abound in the caverns and tunnels. Pelicans, herons, sea gulls, and gannets are commonly seen along the coastline and flamingos frequent isolated lagoons.

The eastern coast is a popular nesting spot for several varieties of marine turtles: hawksbill, loggerhead and green turtles. All of these are protected species, and their nests are carefully tended to so that the offspring can be safely returned to the sea. During turtle season, May through October of 1996 more than 70,000 young turtles were released and estimates for 1997 are 100,000 or more.

An entire book could be written about the marine life alone, but it will be discussed further in a later chapter.

photo 1 The extensive Maracaibo reef zone is the ideal site to spot turtles like this hawksbill that is interrupted from its resting spot by passing divers.

photo 2 Aerial view of the southern part of Cozumel showing the entire Colombia Lagoon and the beaches that skirt the island.

photo 3 The small lagoons on the eastern side of the island are a natural habitat for marine birds, herons and ducks who are commonly spotted feeding there.

photo 4 and 5 Closed to protect and conserve the marine flora and fauna, Colombia Lagoon, now known as Punta Sur Park, is difficult to visit and requires a permit and an official guide.

photo 6 A clear example of the underground rivers of the Yucatan is found in this underground "eye of water" that springs from the subsoil in Colombia lagoon.

foto 7.- Cocopato/White Ibis (Eudocimus albus).

7

4

5

6

Recent investigations date the oldest human remains found in Cozumel around the first years of the Christian era. Although crudely carved stone pieces, glass beads and ceramic fragments have been found, little is known of the men who left their mark but it is speculated that they were isolated groups from Caribbean tribes that occasionally arrived on the island and who were gradually displaced by pressure from more organized and culturally superior groups.

Contrary to accepted beliefs, the Mayans were a seafaring people. In fact, it should be said that they were magnificent mariners who arrived by sea, navigating from fluvial regions of southern Campeche, around the entire Yucatecan peninsula during the 4th century of the Christian era.

The first Mayan group in Cozumel has been identified as part of the Putun-Itzaes, future builders of Chichen-itza, navigators, merchants and warriors who in their travels arrived as far as Central America, embarking from the coast of the Gulf of Mexico.

Having established the island as an important commercial stop, the Putunes-Itzaez increased the population, displacing and eventually eliminating the primitive inhabitants and giving it their own cultural seal, including its Mayan name Cuzaluumil (Cuzam=swallow, Luum=land, Il= pertaining to) which eventually evolved into the present name, Cozumel, land of the swallows.

Although it is possible to find vestiges of the Mayan culture throughout the island, in the interior as well as along the coast, researchers have determined that there were probably at least four principal settlements: Xamancab,

photo 1 A motorcycle tour to the Mayan ruin Caracol is a good way to enjoy the natural beauty of the other side of the island.

photo 2 Covered with sandy mud, a crocodile swims rapidly in the clear waters of Colombia Lagoon.

3

now the city of San Miguel; Tantun-Cuzamil, now known as the archaeological zone of San Gervasio; Oycib, in the southern interior of the island today known as Cedral and Buenavista, on the eastern coast, whose Mayan name has been lost. Each one had a specific function in its age of splendor between the VIII and XII centuries of the Christian era.

4

5

photo 3 The Moreleti crocodile inhabits the southeast of Mexico, Belize and northern Guatemala making its home in large lagoons, savannas and swamplands. A fresh water species, it can grow to lengths of nearly 3 meters.

photo 4 Pedrete Tropical / Pinnated Bittern (Botaurus pinnatus).

photo 5 Chocolatera / Roseate Spoonbill (Ajaia ajaja).

photo 1 Nohoch Nah (Big House). Located on the main Sacbe, this temple marked the entrance to San Gervasio and contained an altar where offerings were made. The entire structure was covered with stucco and painted in shades of red, ochre, and blue. Nohoch Nah was built over two epochs. The first part, comprised of a small platform, went up during the Classic period between 1000-1200 AD. The building we see today, was built on top of it during the Post Classic period of 1200-1650 AD.

Xaman Cab (Northern Land) was the principal port and site of trade for robes, furs, ceramics, jade and volcanic rock jewelry, salt, feathers, fish, etc. The political center was probably located in the city of San Miguel, in the northern area where the air force base is now located.

Tantun - Cuzamil (flat stone of the land of the swallows) was without doubt the religious center. There the temple was raised, a worship site of X'chel, the Mayan goddess of fertility whose principal sanctuary was in Cozumel. Women from all over the Mayan world from the Gulf of Mexico all the way to Central America made pilgrimages to her temple at least once in their lifetime to assure an abundance of offspring without complications in childbirth. The zone is currently known as the San Gervasio Ruins, after a cattle ranch established in the area during the 19th century, unfortunately replacing the original Mayan name.

Oycib (beehive) was the agricultural center and continues to serve as such. It occupies the southern part of the island where water is abundant, the land is fertile and rock outcroppings are minimal. Presently known as El Cedral, it continues to be the agricultural zone of the island, albeit on a much smaller scale.

The Mayan name for what is now called **Buenavista** is unknown. It is situated in the middle of the eastern coastline, facing the Caribbean Sea and appears to have functioned as a maritime signal

foto 2 The Arch. Located in the central part of San Gervasio, on top of the main Sacbe, it signals the way to coastal sites. Pilgrims would bring their offerings to the goddess Ixchel, leaving them on the altar found inside the domed part. Construction is estimated to have taken place during the Post Classic period of 1200-1650 AD.

center and lookout as well as a fisherman's port. Now completely abandoned, the coastal structures have disappeared and the jungle covers or has destroyed the majority of its vestiges.

The conquerors of the era would have been even more astonished, if they had realized the Mayan's scientific advances, their writing system, their astronomical calendar which was superior even to the corresponding European model of that time, and their knowledge of astronomy, that allowed them to discover the orbit of Venus, predict eclipses and even study the movements of Venus. They were also great mathematicians who discovered the concept of zero years before the Europeans and were able to do complicated calculations based on their base 20 numerical system.

photo 3 & 4 Pre-Hispanic structures located on the east side of the island. Castillo Real is the largest of these, and although its purpose remains a mystery, the buildings are believed to have served as navigational aids or lighthouses. They were also used as a place of worship for the sun god Itzamna represented by a beautiful sunset over the Caribbean.

photo 5 Admirable picture of the El Aerolito cenote (sinkhole).

known as **Ik** in his milder form and **Mutulzec** when he was transformed into a hurricane. They also worshipped **Xaman-Ek**, the North Star, goddess of travelers, **Ekchuah**, deity of merchants, **Ah-Puch** god of death and many, many more.

They believed that other worlds and cultures had existed before theirs and were destroyed in a flood. They believed that the world was held up by four guardian brothers, the Bacab, situated in the four compass points and that in the center of the universe (in the world and in their towns) a tree called Yaxch, Sacred Ceiba grew and that its roots held up the heavens and its roots reached all the way to the land of the dead.

They also achieved great advances in medicine and the investigation of medicinal plant properties to the extent that many modern medicines originate from their discoveries.

Their political system was based on a theocratic military model with a social organization made up of marked divisions of the classes. Their religion was polytheistic and inspired by nature. They worshipped the heavenly bodies, the elements, and natural phenomena. Their beliefs were of a dualistic nature, with a clear distinction between good and evil, both equally divine.

Their principle gods were: **Hunab-ku** "one single god" creator of the world and life; **Itzam Na**, god of the heavens, night and day, inventor of writing and the calendar; **Chac**, god of rain and consequently of agriculture; **Yum-Kax**, god of corn and forests and intimately linked to Chac. **X'Chel** or **Ixchel**, wife of Itzam Na, goddess of fertility and pregnancy, of weaving and the moon whose main sanctuary was, as aforementioned, in Cozumel. **Kukulkan**, god of the wind was also

photo 1 Despite mass tourism, the eastern coast of Cozumel remains an inviting place for those wishing to rest and enjoy sun drenched, quiet Caribbean beaches.

The first contact between the Spaniards and the Mayans was a casual one between merchants, (probably from the Yucatan) and the explorer Christopher Columbus during his fourth trip. According to Columbus, this encounter took place on the Guanajas islands in the Gulf of Honduras in 1402.

The Yucatan remained undiscovered by the Europeans, although in 1506, Juan Diaz de Solis and Vicente Yañez Pinzon navigated in front of the eastern coast of the peninsula, without sighting it.

Curiously, the first Spaniards to touch ground on Mayan lands did it without knowing where they were and believing that they had arrived at the bosom of an extraordinary civilization. Those Spaniards were survivors of a shipwreck in 1511 that disembarked from Panama and became stranded on the reefs near Jamaica. Twenty survivors were dragged by the currents to the Yucatecan shores with only 2 surviving until the arrival of the first explorers. They both played an important role in later events. In 1519, Jeronimo de Aguilar, a clergy student became one of the first translators of the conquest. The other, Gonzalo Guerrero, a marine, integrated himself into the Mayan community and achieved a high ranking position amongst the warriors. He married one of the important women of the community and was an author of the fierce indigenous resistance to the conquest.

Although a year earlier, a Spanish expedition from Cuba, under the command of Francisco Hernandez de Cordoba had discovered and claimed the lands of the peninsula for Europe, it was Juan de Grijalva who actually discovered Cozumel. Having set sail from Cuba the first of May in the year 1518, the island was sighted the 3rd of May of the same year, and in accordance with the Catholic Book of Saints given the name, Santa Cruz. After skirting the coastline, they disembarked on the 6th and as was the custom of those times, claimed possession of the new land in the name of the Spanish Monarchy. The chaplain of the expedition, clergyman Juan Diaz Nuñez, held a mass, the first of its kind documented in the history of Mexico, and considered by historians to be the official introduction of Christianity to Mexico. Days later, Grijalva continued his exploration and subsequent discoveries along the peninsular coastline and eventually returned to Cuba, taking information of the new lands he had visited, among them, Cozumel.

photo 2 Punta Chiqueros Reef.

photo 3 Bathers and surfers enjoy the Caribbean Sea on the beaches of Punta Morena.

Motivated by the news and the gold that Grijalva brought back, the governor of Cuba, Diego de Velazquez organized a new expedition, this time with conquest in mind, under the command of Captain Hernan Cortez, a native of Estremadura. Upon departure, the governor tried to remove him from command, fearing that the ambitious Cortez would not include him in the conquest, which was indeed the case.

Cortez left Cuba in February of 1519 and arrived in Cozumel at the end of that month. Because of the hasty

departure to avoid dismissal by Governor Velazquez, he was unaware of exactly what resources, arms and men he had at his disposition and because of this, when he arrived on the beaches of Cozumel, Bernal

photo 3 Cozumel's international airport and world class docking facilities make arrival possible by air or sea.

photo 4 More than 12 scheduled crossings a day from Playa del Carmen keep a constant flow of tourists and goods moving between Cozumel and the mainland. This picture shows the importance of cargo tricycles for transporting merchandise.

photo 1 & 2 Panoramic view illustrating the island's urban and commercial development. Cruise ships call here regularly.

new expedition, under the command of Panfilo de Narvaez, which arrived in Cozumel in February of 1520. The natives, received them kindly as they had the previous navigators, but unfortunately, among the sailors was one infected with smallpox, a disease not yet introduced in the New World and against which the natives had no immunity. The epidemic that ensued among the Mayans of Cozumel caused the death of almost half of the population and consequently initiated the decline of the population of the island which was then further accelerated by the blows of piracy and the indentured slavery imposed upon the natives by the Spaniards.

Dias del Castillo tells us, "he reviewed his troops." He formed squadrons, designated captains, rescued Jeronimo de Aguilar who became his interpreter and after raising an altar and a cross, celebrated the second documented mass on Mexican territory. Having organized and supplied his troops, he set sail for the peninsula and the conquest of Mexico.

The frustrated Governor Velazquez, upon learning of Cortez's betrayal, put together a

photo 5 Sailing ships and large pleasure yachts are a common sight around Cozumel.

photo 6 Sunset on Cozumel Island highlights a view of the cruise ship Costa Romantica.

1

Having consummated the fall of the Aztec Empire, Francisco de Montejo, one of Cortez's captains, wanted to claim his own glory and thus obtained from the Spanish Monarchy, the position of governor of Yucatan. This title authorized him to attempt the conquest of that region, which in spite of being the first discovered by the Spaniards, had still not been dominated.

In 1526, he began his venture, disembarking in Cozumel on September 29 and giving the Mayan pueblo of Xamanca the name San Miguel, a name that it still conserves today. Using the island as a base, he began his penetration of the Yucatan, yet was unable to consolidate his dominion

2

photo 1 *View of the Hotel Zone and the Cozumel International Dock.*

photo 2 *Yucab Reef*

photo 3 *Visitors to Cozumel's eastern shore will find comfort with service at the Playa Bonita Restaurant and beach.*

photo 4 *A diver admires the sponges and sea fans growing along the sides of Jardines de Palancar Reef.*

until 1543, when he founded the cities of Valladolid and Merida, on the settlements of the Mayan towns of Zaci and Th'o.

The island continued to be an arrival point for Spanish ships from Cuba and a provisional base for those on their way to conquests of the peninsula.

It is important to note, that while the Mayans on the continent put up a strong resistance to these conquests, at no time in Cozumel was there an armed fight, perhaps as a consequence of the centuries of pilgrimages that the islanders had become accustomed to and their tradition of receiving and dealing with an assortment of people different from them.

photo 1 Harbor Pilot House.

Achieving the domination of the Mayan region, the Spaniards discovered that the peninsula was lacking in metals of any kind and the land itself was not extremely fertile or productive. The only marketable resource they encountered, was the labor force of the natives themselves, thus a system of slavery known as Encomienda (Concession) was created. Each conqueror was assigned a determined number of natives and a corresponding extension of land and townships, that were in theory, entrusted to his care in exchange for services that they would provide him. He in turn was responsible for their care and instruction in the Catholic religion. In practice, it was purely and simply the legalization of a disguised form of slavery.

In the parceling out of lands, Montejo chose the island of Cozumel, still known as Santa Cruz for himself, but because of protests by some less favored conquerors, he first delegated it under a false name and later, by royal order he left it under the power of the old conqueror, Juan de Contreras, who upon death willed it to his son, Diego Contreras. He in turn held it until 1596,

photo 2 Nightfall from the International Dock and the cruise ship Imagination.

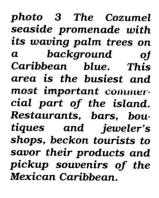

photo 3 The Cozumel seaside promenade with its waving palm trees on a background of Caribbean blue. This area is the busiest and most important commercial part of the island. Restaurants, bars, boutiques and jeweler's shops, beckon tourists to savor their products and pickup souvenirs of the Mexican Caribbean.

when the entire island again fell under direct dominion of the Spanish Monarchy.

The population of the island during this period declined as a result of the disease and the exploitation. The population that had been estimated at 20,000 persons in the 17th century was reduced to a mere 200 individuals. Throughout the following 250 years, the island remained almost deserted, the solitude altered only by the occasional visits of fishermen hunting turtles and sponge or the even more frequent pirate ships that came ashore.

photo 4 Cozumel Island Port Authority building.

Aerial view of the Hotel Zone from north of Cozumel.

The flow of riches that was generated at that time between America and Spain awakened the ambitions of other European nations and gave rise to a pirate trade during the 16th, 17th and 18th centuries in the Caribbean and Atlantic. They roamed the seas in search of Spanish ships, and were not beyond attacking and looting Spanish ports such as Cartagena in Colombia, Panama and Portobello in Panama, Habana in Cuba and Veracruz and Campeche in Mexico.

The first ships were British, protected by the Crown. Soon to follow were the French, the Dutch and on a smaller scale Italian and Portuguese, many of them supported by their governments. Already well accustomed to a life of adventure, they easily assumed

Cruise ships plying the Mexican Caribbean are a mainstay of the island's economy.

the role of pirates making the Caribbean their hunting ground and deserted or scarcely populated islands like Cozumel, their refuge. The frequent visits from pirates to replenish their food and water supply as well as to hide from their possible

captors, contributed to the lack of inhabitants on the island during several centuries

Testament to these days can be found in the many shipwrecks that still remain around the island and the countless stories of treasure that is said to be buried under solitary beaches and in the hidden inlets of the island. The pirates left a legacy of mystery, adventure and romanticism that still fuels treasure hunters on land and sea today in Cozumel.

Vintage Mexican Air Force fighter similar to those used by the 201st Cozumel Squadron during W.W.II.

Characteristic sunset seen from Cozumel's seaside promenade.

Victims of exploitation by the Spaniards since the 16th century, the Mayans watched years pass, without any improvement in their living conditions. For 300 years, with only sporadic, quickly and cruelly squelched rebellions, they were enslaved and forced to work and serve their masters. Even the independence of the country in 1821 didn't improve their plight. All this was what led up to the tragic day of June 30, 1847.

From the very beginning of their independence, peninsular politicians were protagonists in a continuing series of rebellions against the established government in their struggles for power. For many of these rebellions, in order to increase the size of their troops, they enlisted the aid of the natives with promises of lowered taxes, land and better living conditions.

Of course it goes without saying, that none of these promises were carried out when they came into power and many of them actually increased the burden upon the shoulders of the indians, but many of them now had experience in war, among them, an indian chief named Cecilio Chi.

In the year 1847, the patience of the native people had reached its limit and rumors grew of an impending rebellion to be lead by the chief Cecilio Chi. This resulted in an order for his arrest by the armed forces. When he could not be located at his home, his village of Tepich was looted, women were raped and families were killed in retaliation. On July 30, of that tragic year, Cecilio Chi gave a cry for rebellion and attacked the same martyred city where a bloody battle ensued between the white families and the mestizos.

The rebellion spread throughout the eastern peninsula, the rebels collecting a debt for 3 years

photo 1 *View of the ocean promenade and lighthouse at Punta Langosta. In the center of this picture, we can see the Prodive and Aquasafari piers.*

photo 2 *Hard Rock Cafe, on Cozumel's main promenade.*

photo 3 *U.S. franchises like Planet Hollywood can now be found on Cozumel.*

Restaurant Las Palmeras and a view of facilities at the main docking area in the center of San Miguel de Cozumel.

of abuse with a high price in blood and death. One by one the villages fell and in just six months the main city, Valladolid was surrounded and despite a heroic resistance, fell to rebel hands in March of 1848. With this victory, the natives extended their dominion throughout the rest of the peninsula and by May, only Merida and Campeche were still under government control.

The few survivors of the killings in each village, sought refuge far from the theatre of the battle and some of them arrived to the then uninhabited island of Cozumel.

Shot of a Cozumel street with the cruise ship Nieuw Amsterdam in the background.

A colorful Indigo Hamlet decorates the reefs on Cozumel's northern part (Lower Barracuda).

When the War of Independence ended in 1821, a unique character appeared on the beaches of Cozumel. Miguel Molas, a sailor, part merchant and part pirate of Spanish origin had 2 operation centers, one inland, in Chemax near Valladolid and the other on the island, in San Miguel, the ancient Mayan village, where he maintained a small group of agricultural workers.

When the traveler Stephens and his illustrator Catterwood were on the island in 1842 and 1843 they documented seeing only 2 or 3 mestizo families living there.

These were the circumstances of the re-population. Twenty one families arrived around the year 1848 seeking refuge on the island. Their only tools were their hands and their only riches were their hopes for a better life. Years later, new groups increased the budding population. But those twenty one families were the authentic pioneers of the Mexican colonization of the Caribbean, during the years of the Class War.

The growth and consolidation of the new town was rapid. On November 21, 1849, just a year and a half after the arrival of those first pioneers, the Congress of the state of Yucatan, which at that time pertained to what is now Quintana Roo, officially declared the existence of the town of San Miguel at the sight of the ranch of the same name on the western coast

Cautious and solitary during daylight, fragile starfish come out at night in search of food and can often be seen clinging to the sides of sea sponges (Lower Barracuda).

Bird's-eye view of the sheltered Cozumel harbor.

of the island of Cozumel. This same document set the conditions for land grants and established the obligations of the citizens as well as the government.

Fortunately for history's sake, the names of the heads of family who established the foundations for what is today, one of the most important cities in the young state of Quintana Roo, were conserved. The majority of the descendants of the pioneers still live in Cozumel and almost all hold a government post or are business owners.

Wide angled shot of the seaside boulevard seen from the main plaza.

Because they were far from the centers of control of the Yucatan government, they had to stand on their own strength and learn to be self-sufficient not only in their internal government, but also in the elaboration of basic needs such as clothing, shoes, food, etc.

They cultivated and developed their own clothing, music and dance and established their own institutions according to Yucatecan traditions and customs. They created a municipal board in 1852, a

In Cozumel's city center visitors can relax and soak in the tranquil atmosphere that pervades the island and its people.

Beginning with the re-population up until the end of the 19th century, the new residents of Cozumel based their economy on agriculture, without thought to their insular location or the enormous marine wealth available just a hands reach away. They were inland people, farmers, not navigators and they only knew how to live off the land and so that is what they did.

The Plaza Principal or town square, is a gathering place for tourists and locals alike. Here, shoppers can find both domestic and imported products.

civil registry in 1867, and a writing school that same year. At the time of their conception, the rest of what is known today as Quintana Roo was still controlled by Mayan rebels, making these institutions the first and oldest of the state.

Nothing better illustrates the native domination of the continental zone of the peninsula, than the fictional account of Juan Bautista Vega, one of the last Mayan rebel chiefs on the mainland, in spite of having been born and lived his first years on the island of Cozumel.

The Plaza Principal de Cozumel is surrounded by small and picturesque shopping enclaves.

When he was just 10 years old, in 1894, the young Juan Bautista, left school and went with his father who had promised to take 2 foreign missionaries by boat to Tulum. In spite of taking great precautions, they had

Fire spray painting is a popular attraction on downtown streets.

photo 3 A giant Barrel Sponge and a small trunkfish form part of the underwater landscape at Paraiso Reef.

photo 1 Bird's-eye view of the Stouffer Presidente Hotel and Caleta inlet.

photo 2 Dive boats speeding to and from the numerous reefs around Cozumel are a common sight all day long.

scarcely left port when they were attacked by a band of natives. The adults were killed immediately and the boat, after being looted, was burned. The only survivor was the child Juan Bautista, who when he saw a machete about to come down on him, instinctively covered himself with his school books.

He was taken prisoner and brought to the rebel camp and tied to a post for months, fed only the scraps that compassionate children and women would bring him.

Recognizing his ability to read and write, the chief of the Mayan tribe of Champon, took him on as secretary, a position which little by little gained him the trust of his captors. With the passing of time, he adapted completely to the life of the Mayans. He went to combat against the governor with them and quickly rose in the hierarchy of the Mayan rebel military. He married a native and had his own family and when the chief of the tribe died, he was named "general" and head of the group, a position he conserved until his death at a very old age.

photo 4 Adult Stoplight Parrotfish.

When the conflict between the Mayans and the government was over and peace was restored to the region, Juan Bautista, had completely assimilated the lifestyle of the natives and refused to live on the island. Although he occasionally visited his relatives and childhood friends in Cozumel, he chose to live his last days among "his Mayan brothers" as he called them.

photo 5 Grunt Fish and Hog Fish live inside the tunnels formed by Paraiso Reef.

photo 6 A sharp-tailed eel swims away from the advancing photographer (Lower Paraiso).

photo 7 A common scene from beneath the waters of Cozumel. (Paraiso)

With the dawn of the new century, the political and economic climate undertook radical changes. A federal territory was created in 1902 and having established peace with the natives, exploitation of chicle in the interior jungles of the peninsula and the cultivation of coconut along the coast, from Xcalak to Puerto Morelos was initiated.

With the creation of a federal territory, the political system was formalized and as a result, the center of power, moved from the distant Merida, to the somewhat closer Santa Cruz de Bravo, known today as Carrillo Puerto.

Cozumel's economy depends greatly on the regular arrival of great cruise ships that sail around the Caribbean. Forecasts estimate that 1,000 of these vessels, carrying close to one million passengers, will visit the island next year.

Panoramic view of Cozumel on a cruise ship arrival day.

At the same time, the exploitation of the precious woods and chicle of Quintana Roo and the cultivation of coconuts opened new commercial channels. Food, textiles, and drinks were imported from Belize and chicle and copra were exported from Quintana Roo to that British Colony as well as the North American ports of New Orleans and Mobile.

The following pictures give us an idea of the beauty and size of these great ships that tie up at Cozumel.
1. - Carnival Destiny, 2. - Nieuw Amsterdam, 3. - Majestic, 4. - Ecstasy / Leeward, 5. - Celebration, 6. - Royal Majesty, 7. - Britanis, 8. - Majesty of the Sea.

With a 3,000 passenger capacity, the Carnival Destiny is one of the largest cruise ships that calls in Cozumel. The Norwegian Star lies moored next to it.

Pages 40 and 41 The Costa Romantica posed against a magnificent Cozumel sunset.

Another island visitor, the cruise ship Noordam.

Thus, even though the foundation of the economy continued to be agriculture, commercial channels were opened and a new managerial class was born that little by little opened new employment perspectives that strengthened Cozumel throughout the first half of the 20th century making it the most economically active population of the state.

Meanwhile, the city began to consolidate its services. In 1908, public lighting was installed. In 1910 the Governor's Palace was inaugurated along with a city clock. In 1918 the first movie theatre opened as well as mail and telegraph

Celebrity Cruises' "Century" floats on the horizon, resplendent against another beautiful Cozumel sunset.

services. Two years later, electric energy was introduced. In 1924 the first local newspaper began circulation and in 1926 the public library opened its doors. Regular airplane service was inaugurated in 1927.

It was also in these years, that travelers began to discover the island and become its most enthusiastic promoters. Mr. Jose Ma. Pino Suarez, a future vice president of the country was present in the first decade recovering from a serious illness. Years later, the future monarch of Sweden, Gustavo Adolfo, at that time a prince of the crown, also had an extended stay in Cozumel.

Night take of the cruise ships Ecstasy and Leeward tied up at the Cozumel International Dock.

The most famous traveler during that time, was the American aviator Charles Lindbergh who chose Cozumel as one of his stops on his honeymoon trip around the world.

Unfortunately, the economic boom came to a sudden halt at the end of World War II when the market prices

photo 1 A visit to the local museum delivers an interesting history lesson on the origins of the Maya in Cozumel and a modern day perspective of the Spanish conquest.

MUSEO DE LA ISLA DE COZUMEL

Factores que destruyen el arrecife

Factors that destroy the reef

4

first tourism promoter for the island and also the publicity generated by the French explorer Jacques Cousteau. His enthusiastic description of the local reefs changed the economic focus of the islanders from agriculture to tourism and gave birth to the creation of the present tourism industry not only of Cozumel but the entire Mexican Caribbean.

photo 2 This mural in the Cozumel museum depicts a daily scene of Mayan life.

photo 4 Lights on this scale model of Cozumel show the location of the island's most important places.

of Quintana Roo's main exports, chicle and coconut, dropped. In addition, huge hurricanes and prolonged droughts destroyed forests and crops, generating a growing unemployment at the end of the first half of the 20th century.

Fortunately, the commercial vision of the people of Cozumel carried them forward, inspired by the example of the North American, Ilya Chamberlain, the

photos 3, 5 & 6 The Cozumel Island Museum provides fascinating insights into many subjects including the island's origins, wildlife migration patterns, reefs, archeology, galleons and pirates.

5

6

The industry officially commenced operations in the second half of the 50's with the opening of the Hotel Maya Luum (land of the Mayans) by the above mentioned American, Ilya Chamberlain. As activity grew and strengthened, more and more hotels opened which prompted an improvement and increase of collateral services such as car rentals, dive shops, restaurants and transportation companies.

photo 3 Flamboyant (royal poinciana) and Laurel trees provide welcome shade for visitors to the Plaza Principal.

photo 1 On May 6, 1518, just a few steps from the Arcangel Church in the center of Cozumel, a chaplain with the Juan de Grijalva expedition performed the first mass in Mexico. A plaque set at the church's entrance commemorates the details of this important event.

photo 2 The town clock in Juarez Park was built in 1910.

In the sixties, cruise-ships began to stop in Cozumel prompting construction of the first adequate pier in the seventies. Today Cozumel is the principal port of call in Mexico receiving more than 800 ships a year, bringing over a million passengers and making it the second most frequented destination in the Caribbean and fifth in the world market. Although it is now ranked among the most popular sites in Mexico and the Caribbean, Cozumel has

photo 4 Corpuschristi Church on Cozumel Island.

not lost its island charm. In spite of its modern hotels and first class tourist services, the island maintains strong ties to the traditions passed down by the founders of the past century which can be seen throughout the year. Mardi Gras celebrations in February, the Festival of Santa Cruz in May in the small town of Cedral on the south of the island and the Festival of the Patron Saint, San Miguel in September are colorful reminders of the folklore and tradition that are part of Cozumel's past.

All of this, combined with the unlimited natural beauty of its beaches, cenotes, reefs and their strong prehispanic traditions have created a center of tourism that is renowned nationally and internationally. Cozumel has successfully transformed in just a century and a half, what was once just a distant refuge for those fleeing the fury of war into an active city, and a strong pillar of economy for the state.

photo 5 On Sunday nights the town square fills with music and becomes a social gathering place for the inhabitants of Cozumel.

photo 1 Sponges and multicolored corals adorn this colorful image of the Paraiso (Paradise) reef.

Without doubt, the best known attractions of Cozumel Island are her beautiful reefs. With great variety in their formation, setting and the grade or difficulty of visiting them, they are considered an important part of the coral barrier known as the Great Maya Reef. This reef is the second longest in the World and stretches from Contoy Island on the Northeast coast of the Yucatan Peninsula, almost due south to the Gulf of Honduras in Central America.

Because of their exceptional qualities, the reefs of Cozumel enjoy the well deserved fame of being among the best in the World. Contributing to their popularity is the advantage of being able to visit them at any time of year since the water remains transparent with an average temperature between 25°C to 28°C (77°F to 82°F). The average annual

air temperature is approximately 24°C (76°F).

It is also important to consider the marine currents when diving the island. An offshore current of about 2 to 4 knots runs northwards throughout the year and forms the beginnings of the Gulf Stream. Although it comes quite close to the island this does not imply any great risk. To snorkel or dive further from the shore, it is necessary to use support boats to safeguard the people in the water. In diving the coral wall and the shoals, the knowledgeable Cozumel guides add a margin of safety and can find things the tourist would miss. For a visit to the east side and the deep reefs outside the National Park a competent guide is indispensable. The most well known and interesting reefs are the following:

photo 2 Perilously close to the international cruise ship dock, the Paraiso reef shows a great variety of coral formations.

photo 3 The marine fauna of Paraiso include: the Red Hind, the Sharp tailed Eel, and the Hermit Crab.

Paraiso Bajo.- A coral barrier which begins a little beyond the outlet of the Caleta lagoon and runs northwards parallel to the coast almost reaching the international dock. It's maximum depth is 50 feet, with a moderate north bound current. The reef spans 20 to 30 meters and is about a mile long with a maximum height of 4 meters. Composed of little caves and tunnels , the actual structure of the reef is not so impressive, but the marine life is abundant and varied and it is common to find entire families of parrot fish.

photo 4 The Sharp Tailed Eel has a large range of habitat from the sandy shallows covered with grass, to the rocky areas of the reef. Almost without fear of divers, it is possible to get quite close to them until they disappear in the sand or in the caves of the reef.

photo 5 Like a mother watching over her child, this photograph shows us the Florida Horse Conch locally known as Chacpel or Donburro.

49

photo 1 The silhouette of a diver projects from the submarine beauty of the Tormentos reef coral amalgamation.

photo 2 Red Hinds and Moray Eels form part of the marine fauna found on Tormentos reef.

Chankanaab.- Great mounds of coral give the name "Bolones" to this dive site. At a depth of 60 to 70 feet these formations rise from the white seabed up to 25 feet and on their interior wall hang sponges and Gorgonians. In some one may find small trees of black coral. (Look but don't TOUCH!) This is an extensive area which is often visited by enormous grouper who like to rest in the globes of coral unique to this part of the Island.

Tormentos.- This place is famous for the moray eels and grouper which, accustomed to being fed by the divers, come out to inspect them and wait for meal time. The depth is from 60 feet on the sandy bottom to 35 feet at the highest part of the reef. Both novices and advanced divers will enjoy a visit to this colorful habitat.

photo 3 The giant anemone is one of the largest in the Caribbean. Her body and tentacles offer shades of colors through gray, green, brown or yellow. The tentacles are long, with rounded ends which may be pink, yellow, blue or occasionally white. Their habitat in Cozumel embraces the shallow reefs where they are found in the most unexpected positions, to the depths of the wall where they cling as if afraid of falling.

photo 4 A carpet of living colors; in this photo, Tormentos reef reflects the well preserved state in which it is found today.

photo 5 Great Groupers with divers accompanying them are part of the normal scene around Tormentos reef.

Yucab.- One could never have enough bottom time to see all the extraordinary and abundant marine flora and fauna at Yucab. More than a mile of coral formations with a width of 60 to 80 feet cover this extensive and shallow area, making it impossible to enjoy it all on a single tank. The great variety of the bottom life includes corals such as: Brain Coral, Cactus Coral, and Galon some of which are partially covered with Hidroids, Sponges, Worms and Crustaceans.

photo 1 The Yucab reef is considered by some to be a natural aquarium. Along its one mile length live examples of most of the marine flora and fauna of the Island.

photo 2 *The Queen Angel is one of the most colorful fish of the reef.*

photo 3 *Underwater photographers will immensely enjoy a visit to the rainbow world of Yucab.*

photo 4 *A pair of Butterfly Fish hover at the edge of the reef looking for food impervious to the presence of divers.*

photo 5 *The popular Red Hind of the grouper family, form an important segment of Yucab inhabitants.*

photo 6 *The little caves of the reef serve as refuge for the Spiny Caribbean Lobster.*

photo 7 *Also a member the grouper family, the Coney is the most common and most attractive. It is found in reefs close to the coast where it likes to hide inside the caves.*

San Francisco.-The first portion is a vertical wall with encrustations of coral and yellow tubes of large sponges hanging towards the abyss. The depth here starts at 60 to 70 feet with some of the best diving at 120 feet. The wall continues with a slight incline, almost like pasture covered with brilliant green where it is sometimes possible to see large manta rays. The third section is like a ridge of mountains traversed at 70-80 feet by tunnels which bring you up to a platform of sand at only 40 feet. This last site, considered the best part of San Francisco, is comparable with it's famous neighbor, the Santa Rosa reef.

photo 2 The colorful wall of the San Francisco reef is like a brilliant mosaic from which rise corals and tropical fish in their natural glory.

photo 1 In terms of location, the hotel Diamond Cozumel is one of the most privileged of the island. Only a hop, skip and a jump from its fabulous beach are the famous reefs of Santa Rosa and Palancar.

photo 4 Considered a low density hotel which harmonizes with its environment, this picture shows the interior gardens of the Diamond Cozumel, 17 kms. from San Miguel.

photo 5 Protected from the commercial fisheries which almost eliminated them from Caribbean waters, grouper find a safe haven in the Cozumel Marine Reef National Park.

photo 3 There are about 70 species of angel fish which live in tropical and semi-tropical waters around the world. With bodies flattened like vertical discs, their principal food is sponges, although some species also eat seaweed, anemones, gorgonians and small crustaceans. Since they like to travel in pairs, it is thought that these unions are made for life. In this photo we see a pair of gray angel fish.

photo 1 One of the main reasons for diving the Santa Rosa reef is the great quantity of caves and formations which compose this coral barrier. The cave interiors are covered with a profuse variety of corals, fish and sponges of indescribable colors as seen in this photograph of an iridescent french angel fish.

Santa Rosa.- The Santa Rosa wall is considered one of the best dives in the area. Beginning at 50 feet the reef falls to tremendous depths. As one descends, cuts in the wall offer refuge from the pull of the current. In the many caves one may see enormous grouper, soft fans of gorgonians and giant sponges. The average dive here is 80 feet.

photo 2 Protected in the Cozumel reefs, grouper are perhaps the largest and most often observed fish seen in all the dive sites of the Island.

photo 3 & 4 The caves of Santa Rosa have always been a popular attraction. Accustomed to being fed by divers, grouper often follow them in to the caves. In a few of the grottos, one may still find small trees of black coral.

photo pages 56 & 57 One of the truly spectacular denizens of the Caribbean Sea, the Nassau grouper may reach one meter in length and 25 kilos in weight. They seem very curious about divers and frequently follow them. Nassau grouper typically live in reef caves at depths of 40 to 100 feet and are easy to identify from the white vertical bands which cross both sides of its brown body. One finds them in clefts and crevices in the reef awaiting their prey: any fish smaller than they are!

photo 1 A yellow finned grouper comes out of his cave and pleasantly surprises a diver.

Paso del Cedral.- Covered by haphazard patches of coral, the small area of Paso del Cedral houses a submarine community of green eels. Fed and spoiled by the Cozumel guides the eels appear tame to divers. The current here is moderate to strong and the depth is only 60 feet.

photo 2 Many large groupers visit the Paso del Cedral reef, and along with the moray eels which live there, they have also become accustomed to the presence of divers.

photo 3 Careful!!! Not all marine life knows the rules. Some charge out of their caves as divers pass, like this large moray eel confronting an intruder in his domain

photo 1 & 2 At the top of the reef a diver admires the
mixture of gorgonians, anemones, sponges and different
corals. The king angel fish also forms part of the colorful landscape of this site known as Palancar Gardens.

The most famous dive site of the Island is the magnificent mountain of coral known as Palancar. French oceanographer Jacques Ives Cousteau visited Cozumel in 1954 and was amazed by it's beauty. Since then, the Island of Cozumel has become known worldwide and taken it's place as one of the primary dive destinations at the international level.

To dive in Palancar is like flying amongst grand canyons of coral which fall vertically into the undivable depths of the abyss. Monstrous heads of coral climb to 80 feet in height, crowned with red gorgonian fans and enormous yellow sponges. Internal fissures create dramatic passages between the coral mass for the avid diver. The reef system of Palancar is divided according to formation characteristics. The Herradura (the Horseshoe), the Francesa, the Cuevas (Caves) and the Jardines (Gardens) are the most frequently visited.

photo 1 Profusely populated by sea fans, Palancar reef is the ideal place to see these deep water gorgonians in their natural surroundings. They are most often found in large groups crowning the highest parts of the reef. (The Herradura)

photo 2 A shoal of yellow pargo contrasts with pink sponges and the blue of the sea depths in the Jardines de Palancar.

photo 3 A diver enters a cave and enjoys the sight of the great sea fans of Palancar.

photo 4 Some species like the giant barrel sponge may be found only in the depths such as this part of Palancar called the Horseshoe.

photo 5 The varied appearance, textures and colors in the sponge world are truly impressive. Many species of sponges may be found in group formations as if competing for the best position on the reef.

but very worthwhile as the flora are more brilliant and colorful than elsewhere. Dive depth here is 60 to 70 feet in the higher part of the ranges and 90 to 110 feet at the sandy bottom.

The palisade is irregular, tending towards the vertical in some parts. Inside the caves, as on the rest of the Island, one finds large sponges, gorgonian fans, and different corals. close to the coast is a range at a depth of only 40 feet known as the Bajo of Punta Sur (Punta Sur Shoals) which one can enjoy with only snorkel, mask and fins.

photo 1 A tiger grouper emerges from a submarine passage in this shot from Punta Sur.

Punta Sur.- Situated between the reefs of Columbia and Maracaibo, the reef ecosystem named Punta Sur is one of the deepest and most impressive dives on Cozumel. Here exists the famous Garganta del Diablo (Devil's throat) where the diver enters the mouth of a cave at only 50 feet and exits into the abyss at 130 feet. One must use flashlights and a guide with the experience for this type of dive. Similar to the Palancar reef but with more depth in the caves, the Punta Sur reefs are less visited than others

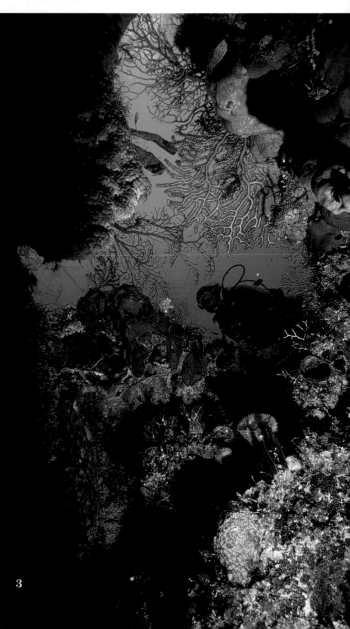

photo 2 The extensive reefs of Cozumel are the dwellings for a great diversity of marine life including the great barracuda.

photo 3 & 4 Of enormous dimension and unique characteristics, the caves of Punta Sur reef are visited by large grouper and divers who find the interiors covered by giant sponges, sea fans and an indescribable variety of marine flora and fauna.

1

2

3

Probably the least frequented of the Island reefs are those of Maracaibo which are found to the south. They are further off shore and therefore more exposed to the southeast winds. Sometimes the ocean swells make them uncomfortable and even dangerous to visit. When conditions are right, it is still possible to meet with large manta rays, turtles and nurse sharks resting in the small caves. Moreover, there is a second "Devil's Throat" with the difference that this one opens like a window looking out to sea from a depth of 130 feet.

photo 1 Coralscapes of indisputable beauty are the principal attraction of the deep reefs of Maracaibo, at the southern end of the Island.

photos 2 & 3 The king crab and the spiny Caribbean lobster are permanent residents of the Maracaibo shoals.

The wall dive is very deep, and in some parts breaches and tunnels of great beauty descend to the profound blue; and without noticing, a diver may reach 150 feet.

The northerly set of currents sweep both sides of the Island, bringing plankton and nutrients which create an abundance of sea life and the special colors of the reefs in this area. A shallower dive of 60 to 80 feet can be made on the extensive ridge of the Maracaibo Shoals, also called Chunchakab. It zigzags northwards from Punta Sur in disorderly fashion for almost a mile towards Punta Celarain.

All these sites, from Barracuda to Maracaibo form the Cozumel Marine Reef National Park which was established in 1996 in order to prevent the depredation of the flora and fauna which have made the Island so famous, enticing thousands of divers each year.

Another reason for the Marine Park is to regulate the personnel and diveboats with regard to the use, protection and conservation of reef resources, and the safety of services offered to tourism in general.

On the east coast of the Island exist a number of interesting sites such as: Islote, Chen Rio, Chiqueros, San Martin and the micro atolls of Hanan. These last are similar in form to South Pacific atolls and are the only formations of this type in the Mexican Caribbean.

photo 4 A diver admires and enjoys the gentle presence of a trumpetfish gracefully cruising the southern reefs.

photo 5 A hawksbill turtle is startled by passing divers.

photo 6 A nurse shark rest in a cave among the corals.

1

2

photo 1 To rest in the shade of a palm tree, snorkel in crystal clear waters and enjoy fresh seafood by the sea; these are attractions for both the visitor and Island

century, it contains examples of past grandeur despite centuries of abandonment, jungle encroachment, hurricanes and acts of vandalism at the hands of human beings.

In recent years, institutions such as the Peabody Museum of the USA and the National Institute of Anthropology and History of Mexico, have carried out restorations and a portion of the archeological zone has been opened to the public. The Island Foundation of Parks and Museums staffs an information booth with tourist services and they are in the process of consolidating an on site mini-museum. There are bilingual guides available to give explanations of

photo 2 The Maya ruin known as the "Caracol" is situated on the road to Punta Celarain lighthouse.

Although there exist vestiges of the ancient and grand Maya culture all over the Island, one of the sites best known for the quantity and conservation of its buildings is the prehispanic settlement of San Gervasio. A religious center of the Maya since the 8th

the architectural, historical

3

photo 3 Destroyed by centuries of bad weather, the colored ancient Maya designs of San Gervasio are now more difficult to appreciate than when they were in their full glory.

photo 4 The Castillo Real is the largest and best preserved of the Maya temples of the Caribbean coast.

4

locals at the bathing resort of Chen-Rio on the east coast of Cozumel Island.

and cultural significance of the archaeological zone.

A human settlement for more than a 1,000 years, el Cedral known in Maya times as Oycib, preserves it's agricultural tradition and guards within its grounds some vestiges of Maya constructions from the so-called "decadent" period, of approximately the XII century AD.

The Caracol is one of the best conserved remains. It lies to one side of the Punta Celarain lighthouse road on the south point of the Island. Ten centuries ago it is possible that this was an altar for offerings and a watch tower for signaling Maya maritime traffic.

photo 5 Another important public beach on the Island is the resort of Playa Sol whose attractions include aquatic sports, wide white coral sand beaches and local food.

The northeast coast of Cozumel boasts several Maya temples close to the sea. By far the largest is the Castillo Real (Royal Castle), a little more than 10 kms. north of Mezcali-tos. To reach it requires a four wheel drive vehicle. Semi-destroyed by the hurricanes of 1967, 1988, and 1995, it was possibly a lighthouse or temple dedicated to storms and the sun.

Surrounded by the waters of the Rio de la Plata lagoon and almost covered by jungle, there are ruins at the north of the island which communicate with San Gervasio by means of a Sac-be; Maya for "white road".

photo 6 One of the most famous and frequented beaches in Cozumel is the San Francisco Park near the southern end of the Island.

photo 1 Each night during Carnival, the Benito Juarez park is converted into a grand popular party and is the meeting place for tourists and the local community.

On the southeast tip of the Island, within easy access, stands the Punta Celarain lighthouse. The oldest on Cozumel, dating from the 1930's, it replaces one built in the past century. Thirty meters in height, the powerful light dominates all the Punta Sur Park, Columbia and the southern approach to the Island.

The northern approaches to the island are signaled by the Punta Molas lighthouse. More modern than Punta Celarain, it is distinguished by its red tower rising to a height of 28 meters. Difficult to reach by road, one may be permitted to ascend the tower and contemplate the lagoons of Rio de la Plata and Montecristo.

The San Miguel lighthouse stands to the south of the town. Relatively new, its light at a height of 15 meters is obscured to the north & south by more modern buildings. The principal purpose of this navigational aid is to signal the main approach to the town across Cozumel Channel.

With a few more than 60,000 inhabitants San Miguel is the only real population center of the Island and third largest in the state. In general a clean town, it is characterized by it's tranquillity and security. Some buildings from the last century are preserved, such as Palomar at the crossroads of the Malecon (seawall) and street #10, the Alemanes in the city center, and a few private homes.

Parque Juarez is the principal square on the Island and its position opposite the arrival dock for Cozumel makes it a convergence spot for Islanders & visitors alike. A stop at the Museum of the Island of Cozumel should not be missed. The same is true for the National Park at Chankanaab. As Cozumel is a population with centuries of history, her customs and traditions span several cultures which give pleasant variety to

photo 2 The costumed groups and their dances bring tropical flavor and colorful gaiety to the Carnival parties.

the popular fiestas as demonstrated in the distinctive dress and dances and foods.

The fiesta of Carnival is a movable feast usually celebrated during February. The tradition began in the last century with deep roots in the community so that nearly all the inhabitants participate, making streets and plazas into party halls. Especially notable are the groups in masquerade, dancing through the streets. Comprised of people of all ages, they form the main procession of decorated floats along the Malecon.

photo 3 & 4 The procession of decorated floats includes themes which may represent the submarine life of the island or tropical landscapes with handsome costumed dancers and performing artists.

the Cabeza de Cochino y las Cintas (Head of the Pig and the Ribbons), which is presented the afternoon of the 3rd of May, the day of Santa Cruz (Holy Cross).

The fiesta of San Miguel is celebrated in honor of the patron of the town and takes place in September with religious and popular ceremonies.

The celebration known as the "Day of the Dead" is held at the beginning of November and is a homage to the deceased with prayers and offerings of food. Most notable are the "Altars of the Dead" built with folk art, foods and colored candles.

The Christmas festival proceeds with Posadas. This is a tradition of the Catholic church inherited from Spain. Children carry a decorated branch from house to house, singing and asking favors. There is caroling in the squares, and lights and decorations in the houses and city streets.

The Cedral Fair is celebrated in the first days of May in the town of that name. With 150 years of tradition, it originates from the "War of the Castes" in Yucatan. One of the survivors who took refuge on Cozumel, swore an oath to pay homage to the Cross for the rest of his life and the lives of his descendants. Now transformed into an agricultural, commercial and cultural fair it still preserves some of the Maya tradition in the ancestral dances such as

photo 5 Live music and open air dancing are the most popular expressions of Carnival in Cozumel.

A beautiful view of the Malecon bathed in the colors of sunset.

Transport to and from the island is ample and varied. Since it is an island, sea is the most usual mode, with 2 routes available: a passenger ferry from Playa del Carmen (18 kms.) with continuous crossings all day; or one from Puerto Morelos, 40 kms. to the north of Playa del Carmen, for vehicles and passengers, with one crossing a day.

Cozumel's international airport receives several domestic flights daily from Mexico, Merida, Playa del Carmen and Cancun, with international flights from Houston and Miami. There are also many charter flights from other cities in the USA and Canada.

One has the option to travel on one of the great cruise ships from Miami, Florida, to Cozumel with stops in the Bahamas, Santo Domingo, Jamaica and the Caymans.

Cozumel has had a postal service since the last century and telegrams since 1910. The Island is fully integrated into the national communications network. There is international fax service from the telegraph office. The local telephone service is reliable with good national and international connections, the long distance code from the USA being 01-987.

1

2

qualified staff to attend the cases of decompression sickness which may occur when diving at the greater depths without taking the proper precautions.

Moreover, both the firefighters and the Red Cross are prepared with trained paramedics and the equipment to attend emergencies. Since San Miguel is the Island's principal population center, all civil and emergency services are based there. In addition to its public security force and traffic control, the municipality has the tourist police, a bilingual group created to attend, orientate and help visitors.

Island health services are dependable, however they are limited in their specialties. Private clinics also are of a good standard. To accommodate divers, there are 3 hyperbaric chambers with

photo 1 View of the rocky coast of Chankanaab with a background of cruise ships.

photo 2 The introduction to the underwater world of Chankanaab is a favorite activity for people of all ages.

photo 3 The Chankanaab lagoon originates from the erosion of the calciferous rock by the forces of rain and sea water. It is considered a world class ecosystem of unique interest.

The great influx of the sea allows the formation of corals in the lagoon interior and the development of a large community of marine life which depends on communication with the sea by two underwater caverns.

3

Local security is augmented by the presence of both Mexican Air Force and Navy detachments on the Island. One may rest assured that vigilance, police assistance, and emergency preparedness on Cozumel function at a higher level than the national average.

One must not forget the public services. Both street cleaning and garbage collection ere excellent and contribute to the good image and general health of the Island.

photos 4, 5, 6, & 7 Colorful reefs and extensive marine life are the attractions of the Chankanaab shoals. As examples we have the yellow ray and the small drum.

In the deepest parts of the reef, king angel fish and yellow pargo adorn the walls of the site known as the "Bolones of Chankanaab".

Another important service is that of parks and gardens. The municipality has it's own nursery for reforestation and the gardeners keep the parks attractive and the avenues aglow with trees.

In line with it's position as a first class tourist attraction, Cozumel offers numerous four and five star hotels on the beach, and some of the three and four star category downtown. In total there are more than 4000 rooms. Five hundred additional hotel accommodations are under construction on the south coast.

Tourism via cruise ships brings the largest flow of visitors to Cozumel and the frequency of the arrival of these giants of the sea, more than eight hundred per year, makes the Island Mexico's premier cruise ship terminus. Cozumel is in the top five leading Caribbean cruise ship destinations and seventh in the world.

photo 1 Aerial view of the Chankanaab National Park.

To supply docking services and transport facilities to visiting cruise ships, the Island has one pier with two mooring positions in service, another now being finished with two more positions which will come on line in late 1997, and a third under construction which will be ready for 1999. Each includes land installations to attend the passengers comprising: souvenir shops, restaurants, bars, and information offices.

For transferring visitors to points of interest, the Island counts on three hundred taxis and twenty suburbans for special services. All prices are government controlled. Car hire is also available from companies such as Avis, Hertz, Dollar, Budget etc.

Diving is undoubtedly the leading recreational pastime on the Island. With so many sites, both for snorkeling and diving, this has become an activity enjoyed all year round.

photos 2, 3, & 5 A walk through the archeological zone of Chankanaab shows the visitor marvelous prehispanic replicas exhibited there which represent the principal Meso-american cultures.

photos 4 & 6 Large, colorful iguanas live around the lagoon and the botanical garden.

photo 7 In the Maya language, Chankanaab means "little sea" and a visit to this natural reserve will be an unforgettable pleasure.

The park contains a botanical garden with more than 400 species of native plants, a "Zona Maya" which demonstrates the development of the ancestral culture, and also a museum full of information about the terrestrial flora, fauna, and marine life of the region.

The dive shops offer training courses and certification from beginners to advanced divers with professional instructors and bilingual guides.

Sport fishing is yet another reason to come to Cozumel. The International Billfish Tournament takes place in May for sailfish and marlin. Anglers from all over Mexico, Cuba and the USA congregate on the Island for the fishing and a world famous fiesta which lasts a week. The Cozumel event forms a circuit with Puerto Aventuras on the coast and the Annual Isla Mujeres Red Cross Tournament also in May. Other tournaments, more local in nature, take place in the first days of June, in September, and November.

The beaches of the Island are enough in their own right to make Cozumel a first class tourist attraction.

To the brilliant and transparent waters of the Caribbean, add the almost permanent calm of the waters on the west coast, and one can appreciate that there are few places in the world so geographically privileged as this island. Here also, are the beautiful beaches such as Playa Azul, 4kms north of the city, Ceiba, next to the international dock, and Uvas 6 kms. south of the city. Chankanaab Botanical and Underwater Park deserves special mention. Playa Corona, Playa Maya, Santa Maria, San Francisco, Playa Sol, the Paso del Cedral, the Francesa, and Palancar follow each other to form a rosary of the sea, sand and sun for lovers of nature.

For those interested in cultural activities, the Island museum offers various artistic exhibitions, permanent and short term, theater activities, painting courses, ecological orientation, and several activities for children,

photo 1 Dawn on the east coast of Cozumel from the road to Punta Molas lighthouse.

photos 2 & 3 Free diving makes it possible for almost anyone to admire the underwater marvels of the Cozumel reefs.

as well as an introduction to Island origins, history and development.

Additionally, the Quintana Roo Institute of Culture offers courses of dance, painting, music, and theater within the official sphere, and the privately funded Ixchel Cultural Institute offers classes of different artistic activities and programs periodic exhibitions of works having artistic or historical value.

The International Festival of Dance brings groups of local and North American artists together in July. The Festival

foto 4. El Islote reef.

of Caribbean Culture in October/November presents dance spectaculars and music from the countries of the Caribbean Basin: Cuba, Haiti, Dominican Republic, Puerto Rico, Venezuela, Aruba, Columbia, Costa Rica, Panama, Honduras, Guatemala, Belize, and of course Mexico.

Part of the rich cultural heritage of Mexico, on Sunday afternoons in the main square it is possible to admire concerts by school groups who cultivate traditional folk dancing from different regions throughout the country.

We hope that this book has served you as a guide and souvenir of your visit to the Island and has shown in these images something of the great Maya culture that thrived here in times past. That you carry with you the customs and traditions of her people today, the beauty of the underwater flora and fauna, her beaches and lagoons, her modern attributes including San Miguel, the sea-side hotels, and the majestic cruise ships which have chosen Cozumel as their principal destination, an exquisite jewel afloat in the Mexican Caribbean.

photo 5 A pod of bottle nosed dolphin is captured on film as they pass by the Island of Cozumel.

Published by
EDITORA FOTOGRAFICA MARINA KUKULCAN S.A. DE C.V.
Kabah Ave. 24 S.M.31 Zip Code 77508 Cancún Quintana Roo, México. Ph./Fax.:01(98) 87-47-68

Editor & Photographer
LUIS GÓMEZ CÁRDENAS

Artwork
JAVIER ORTIZ SILVA

Assistant Editors
PROF. VELIO VIVAS VALDÉS
General information about the island of Cozumel.

LUIS GÓMEZ CÁRDENAS - *The underwater world*

MICHAEL CREAMER - *Introduction, translation*

DENISE FULLERTON DE GÓMEZ
Spanish-English translation

Editorial Acknowledgements
PROF. VELIO VIVAS VALDÉS
Cozumel's lifetime chronicler and historian.

Printed by
Kina Italia S.p.A. - Milan, Italy

ISBN - 968 - 7782 - 01 - 3